THE WAR OF 1812

By the Dawn's Early Light

Heather E. Schwartz

Consultants

Vanessa Ann Gunther, Ph.D.
Department of History
Chapman University

Nicholas Baker, Ed.D.
Supervisor of Curriculum and Instruction
Colonial School District, DE

Katie Blomquist, Ed.S.
Fairfax County Public Schools

Publishing Credits

Rachelle Cracchiolo, M.S.Ed., *Publisher*
Conni Medina, M.A.Ed., *Managing Editor*
Emily R. Smith, M.A.Ed., *Series Developer*
Diana Kenney, M.A.Ed., NBCT, *Content Director*
Courtney Patterson, *Senior Graphic Designer*
Lynette Ordoñez, *Editor*

Image Credits: Cover and p. 1 Bridgeman Images; p. 4 (left) Walters Art Museum, Baltimore, USA/Bridgeman Images, (right) Courtesy of the Maryland Historical Society, Item 54315; p. 5 Christie's Images/ Bridgeman Images; p. 6 The Crown Estate/Bridgeman Images; p. 7 Chateau de Versailles, France/Bridgeman Images; pp. 8, 10, 13, 16, 27 North Wind Picture Archives; p. 9 LOC [LC-USZC4-6235]; p. 10 Peter Newark American Pictures/Bridgeman Images; pp. 10-11 LOC [LC-DIG-pga-01891]; p. 12 Bureau of Engraving and Printing/Wikimedia Commons; p. 13 Kean Collection/Hulton Archive/Getty Images; p. 14 Gilder Lehrman Collection, New York, USA/Bridgeman Images; p. 15 (top) American Antiquarian Society, Worcester, Massachusetts, USA/ Bridgeman Images; pp.15 (bottom), back cover Creative Commons James C. Orvis, used under CC BY-SA 4.0 https://goo.gl/Lbp4OW; p.17 Bettmann/Getty Images; p.17 LOC [LC-DIG-ppmsca-2307]; p.18 Collection of the New-York Historical Society, USA/Bridgeman Images; p.19 Picture History/Newscom; p.20 NARA [5730368]; p.21 Special Collections Toronto Public Library / Flickr License: Creative Commons BY-SA 2.0; p.23 Universal History Archive/UIG via Getty Images; p.24 Look and Learn/Bridgeman Images; p.25 Bridgeman Images; p.27 (front) LOC [2014571450], (back) GraphicaArtis/Bridgeman Images; p.31 Walters Art Museum, Baltimore, USA/Bridgeman Images; p.32 Courtesy of the Maryland Historical Society, Item 54315; all other images from iStock and/or Shutterstock.

Library of Congress Cataloging-in-Publication Data

Names: Schwartz, Heather E., author.
Title: The War of 1812 : by the dawn's early light / Heather E. Schwartz.
Description: Huntington Beach, CA : Teacher Created Materials, 2017. | Includes index. | Audience: Grade 4-6.
Identifiers: LCCN 2016034138 (print) | LCCN 2016040011 (ebook) | ISBN 9781493837946 (pbk.) | ISBN 9781480757592 (eBook)
Subjects: LCSH: United States--History--War of 1812--Juvenile literature.
Classification: LCC E354 .S479 2017 (print) | LCC E354 (ebook) | DDC 973.5/2--dc23
LC record available at https://lccn.loc.gov/2016034138

Teacher Created Materials

5301 Oceanus Drive
Huntington Beach, CA 92649-1030
http://www.tcmpub.com

ISBN 978-1-4938-3794-6

Table of Contents

The War That Inspired an Anthem

As a battle raged during the War of 1812, Francis Scott Key looked out his window. He saw the American flag raised high and proud over Maryland's Fort McHenry. He was overcome. He knew this meant the Americans at the fort had refused to surrender to British soldiers. The United States was victorious at Fort McHenry. A sense of pride ran through him.

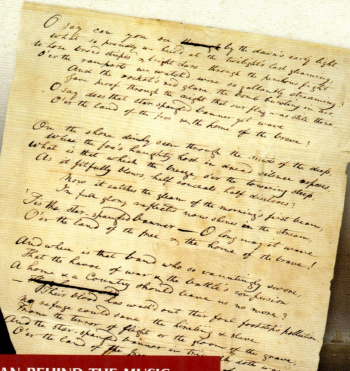

Francis Scott Key and original draft of his poem

THE MAN BEHIND THE MUSIC

Francis Scott Key went to Maryland during the War of 1812 to negotiate the release of a man who was being held by the British. He was successful but, he was later **detained** while Fort McHenry was under attack.

4

Key began to write. His words spilled out on the back of a letter. His poem would later become the country's national **anthem**, "The Star-Spangled Banner."

> *O! say can you see by the dawn's early light,*
> *What so proudly we hailed at the twilight's last gleaming,*
> *Whose broad stripes and bright stars through the perilous fight,*
> *O'er the ramparts we watch'd were so gallantly streaming?*
> *And the Rockets' red glare, the Bombs bursting in air,*
> *Gave proof through the night that our Flag was still there;*
> *O! say does that star-spangled Banner yet wave,*
> *O'er the Land of the free, and the home of the brave?*

In the early 1800s, the United States found itself at war with Great Britain once again. The nation was fighting for the freedom it had won in the American Revolution. But could the young country survive another war?

Battle of Fort McHenry

5

Why War?

The road to war was a bumpy one. Many Americans did not wish to go to war with Great Britain. But a series of events and policies made leaders reconsider.

Trouble Trading

The Napoleonic wars raged among France, Great Britain, and many other countries in Europe. This series of wars began in 1803 and ended in 1815. It was a continuation of a larger conflict in Europe. While at war, both the French and the British wanted to harm the other by blocking trade. The United States tried to remain **neutral**. However, both other countries made this impossible. Each passed laws to stop the United States from trading with the other. These laws hurt the U.S. **economy**.

The British defeat France and Spain during the Battle of Trafalgar.

In 1806, France issued the Berlin Decree. It said American ships that went to British ports were *not* neutral. They were enemies of France. Later, in 1807, Great Britain issued the Orders in Council. This required American ships to get licensed and pay a tax at British ports before going to France. But, they had to violate the Berlin Decree to do so. The United States was caught in the middle.

Napoleon and his troops defeat Russia at the Battle of Friedland.

NAPOLEON SEIZES POWER

In the early 1800s, France was in turmoil. They had been fighting the French revolutionary wars. During this time, **dictator** Napoleon Bonaparte (BOH-nuh-part) rose to power. The Napoleonic wars began as he tried to expand his empire.

Impressment

Americans were upset about the restrictions on trade. But they were also angry over a British policy called **impressment**. The British forced sailors off American ships to serve in the British Royal Navy. Some sailors were British **citizens** who had **deserted** the Royal Navy. They did not want to fight in Europe's wars. Others were American citizens. Regardless, if sailors could not prove they were American, the British captured them.

President Thomas Jefferson wanted to protect American sailors. He also wanted to punish Great Britain and France. He signed the **Embargo** Act in 1807. It stopped almost all American trade. He hoped that it would make Great Britain and France lose money. But, it hurt the United States more than it hurt the other countries.

A sailor is forced to serve in the British military.

This 1808 political cartoon shows Jefferson addressing complaints about the Embargo Act.

Congress replaced the law in 1809. This new law was called the Non-Intercourse Act. It forbade trade with Great Britain and France. But, it allowed the United States to trade with other countries. This law was not successful either. American merchants broke the law to trade with the British and the French. In 1810, Congress and President James Madison passed another trade law. But it also failed to help the United States.

Some congressmen were fed up. They wanted to go to war and quickly earned the nickname, "War Hawks." Tensions continued to rise as the British captured thousands of sailors. The French also seized American ships. This pushed the United States closer to war.

Conflicts with American Indians

In the early 1800s, Americans also wanted to expand the country. They pushed into American Indian land. The British knew tribes worried about losing their homes. They encouraged tribes to fight back.

Tecumseh (tuh-KUHMP-suh) and his brother, Tenskwatawa (ten-SKWAH-tuh-wah), were American Indian leaders. They worked to unite many tribal nations. They wanted to stop people from taking over their lands.

Tecumseh

Tenskwatawa

The two men gathered an army of American Indians. While Tecumseh was away in 1811, his brother was left in charge of their army. Tenskwatawa heard that U.S. soldiers were near his people. He wanted to strike first. So, he sent his army into the Battle of Tippecanoe. They attacked U.S. troops, but they were forced to retreat and lost the battle.

Tecumseh returned to a much weaker army. He saw that his people could not defeat the United States. So, they joined forces with Great Britain. With tribes siding with the British, U.S. leaders saw further cause to declare war.

War Hawks kept calling for war. They wanted Great Britain to stay out of their business. Madison agreed. He thought it was time to fight.

Battle of Tippecanoe

The United States Goes to War

President Madison addressed Congress, urging it to declare war on Great Britain. On June 18, 1812, Congress did just that. The War of 1812 had begun.

Meanwhile, in Europe, the British were busy fighting France. The country's leaders thought that war was more important. They thought the war with the United States was more of a nuisance. American leaders felt differently. They were eager to fight. They wanted to guard their rights and prove their independence.

U.S. General William Hull led troops from Detroit to **invade** Canada and seize land. Many American leaders, such as Thomas Jefferson, thought the attack on Canada was a sure win. Jefferson wrote, "The **acquisition** of Canada this year, as far as the neighborhood of Quebec, will be a mere matter of marching and will give us experience for the attack of Halifax the next, and the final **expulsion** of England from the American continent."

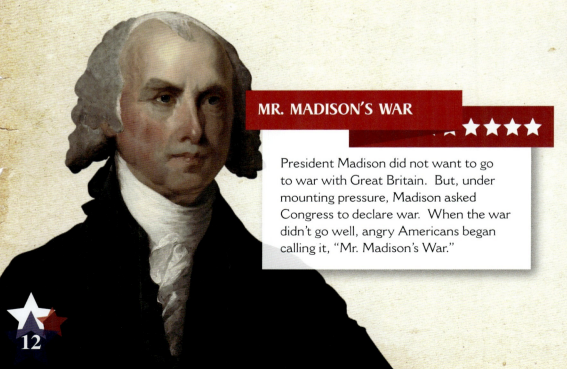

MR. MADISON'S WAR

★★★★

President Madison did not want to go to war with Great Britain. But, under mounting pressure, Madison asked Congress to declare war. When the war didn't go well, angry Americans began calling it, "Mr. Madison's War."

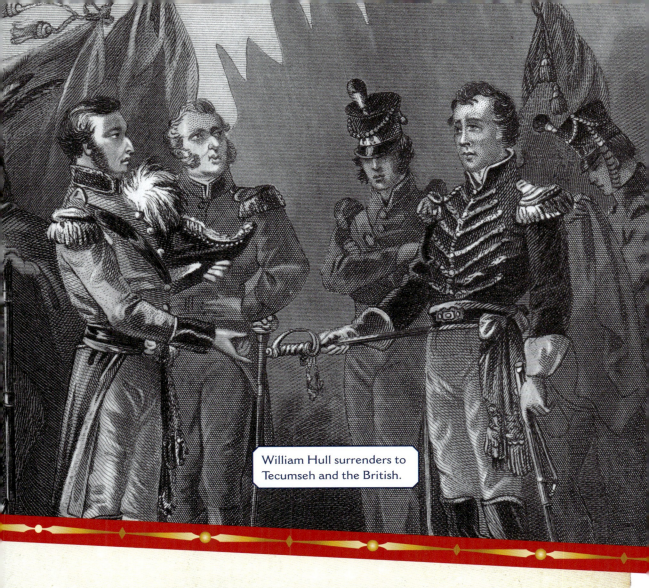

William Hull surrenders to Tecumseh and the British.

U.S. leaders had high hopes. But, the attempt did not go as planned. British soldiers and Tecumseh's army were prepared. They pushed U.S. forces back across the border and seized American forts and supplies. They tricked Hull into thinking they were outnumbered. Fearing defeat, Hull surrendered.

The United States did not gain land in Canada as planned. It lost Detroit without a single shot being fired. The country was disgraced. Hull was **court-martialed** for his mistakes.

The war continued into 1813. The United States won other battles. In April, U.S. troops beat the British in the Battle of York. They also burned the city, which served as Canada's capital.

In September 1813, nine U.S. ships fought six British ships. They met on Lake Erie, off the coast of Ohio. The British had better weapons. Their guns could shoot cannonballs almost one mile (1.6 kilometers). The Americans had guns that could only shoot about half a mile (0.8 km). For hours, the wind kept U.S. forces from getting close enough to attack. Seizing their chance, the British fired for hours upon one of the U.S. ships. They virtually destroyed it. Finally, the wind shifted. American troops were within range for an attack. The battle ended in a U.S. victory. The United States reclaimed Detroit.

Battle of Lake Erie

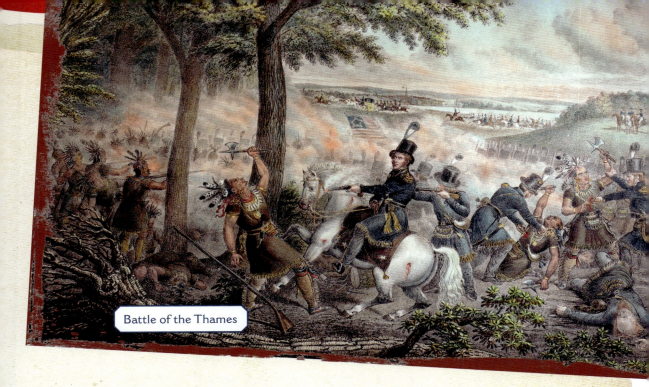

Battle of the Thames

In October 1813, Americans fought the British in the Battle of the Thames (TEMZ). The two sides met in Ontario, Canada. The British had 600 troops on their side. Tecumseh and about 1,000 warriors fought for them, too. But, the United States brought about 3,500 troops. They quickly beat the British and their **allies**. Tecumseh died in battle. When the tribes lost their leader, they ended their alliance with the British.

ULTIMATE SACRIFICE

Many people lost their lives during the War of 1812. In the Battle of the Thames, there were 45 American, 80 British, and at least 33 American Indian **casualties**. By the end of the war, thousands of soldiers had died.

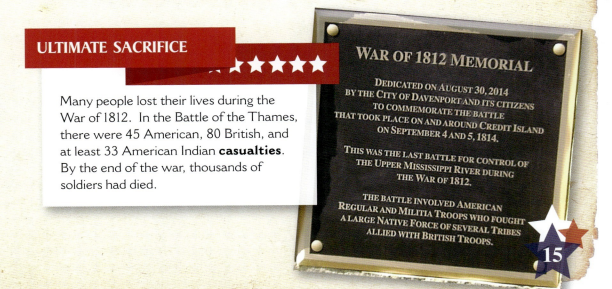

WAR OF 1812 MEMORIAL

DEDICATED ON AUGUST 30, 2014 BY THE CITY OF DAVENPORT AND ITS CITIZENS TO COMMEMORATE THE BATTLE THAT TOOK PLACE ON AND AROUND CREDIT ISLAND ON SEPTEMBER 4 AND 5, 1814.

THIS WAS THE LAST BATTLE FOR CONTROL OF THE UPPER MISSISSIPPI RIVER DURING THE WAR OF 1812.

THE BATTLE INVOLVED AMERICAN REGULAR AND MILITIA TROOPS WHO FOUGHT A LARGE NATIVE FORCE OF SEVERAL TRIBES ALLIED WITH BRITISH TROOPS.

In 1814, the British headed to Washington, DC. They were angry over the burning of York from the year before. They wanted revenge. Most **civilians** left the city in fear. They escaped to friends' homes in other cities. Some even hid in the woods. The city was defenseless against British troops.

The British set fire to the U.S. Capitol. It housed the Library of Congress, the House of Representatives, the Senate, and the Supreme Court. They set fire to the President's House (later called the White House). Documents, monuments, and art all went up in flames. The fire was intense. Americans watched in horror as their capital city burned. They could see the blaze from as far as 50 miles away. The British military raised Great Britain's flag over the United States' capital. It was a sad and terrifying sight for the young country.

DOLLEY SAVES GEORGE

First Lady Dolley Madison helped save several items from the President's House before it was burned. One of the most important pieces was a portrait of the country's first president, George Washington. She ordered servants and an enslaved man named Paul Jennings to remove and preserve the painting.

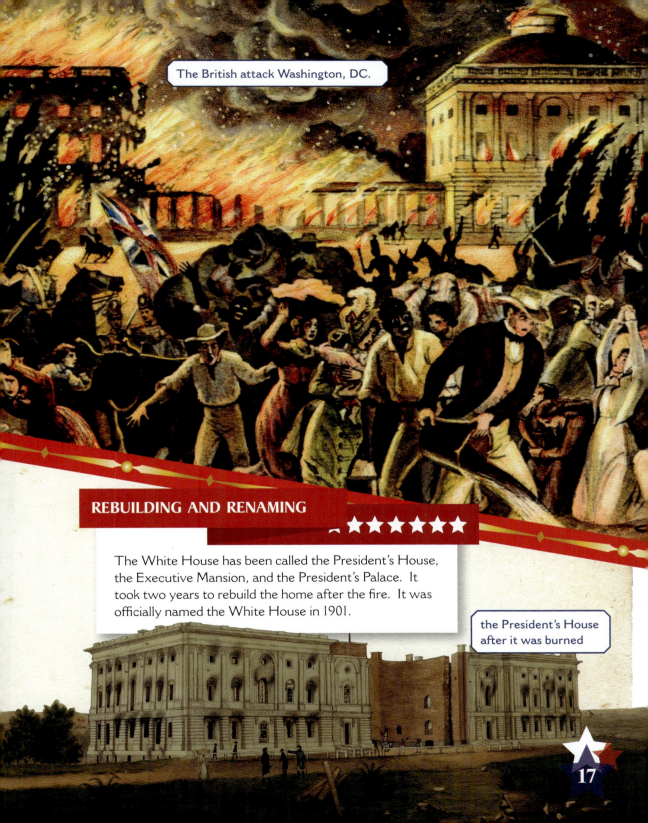

The British attack Washington, DC.

REBUILDING AND RENAMING

The White House has been called the President's House, the Executive Mansion, and the President's Palace. It took two years to rebuild the home after the fire. It was officially named the White House in 1901.

the President's House after it was burned

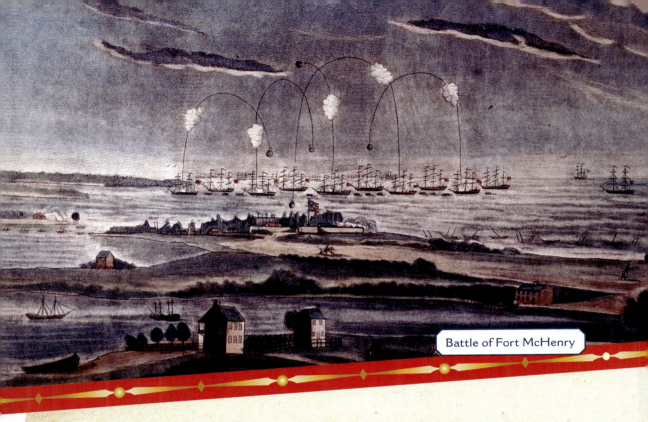

Battle of Fort McHenry

Less than a month after the British burned the capital, the situation did not look good for the United States. On September 12, 1814, a fleet of British ships arrived off the coast of Maryland. About 4,500 British soldiers marched into Baltimore. Other British troops remained on the ships. They planned to attack by land and sea.

At 6:30 a.m. on September 13, the ships began firing at Fort McHenry. About 1,000 U.S. troops tried to fight back, but their weapons could not fire far enough to reach the ships.

This is the battle Francis Scott Key watched. He had no idea how it might end. Would Fort McHenry be forced to surrender? Would the United States lose the war? What would that mean for the nation?

These questions were answered on the morning of September 14. Key saw proof of U.S. victory. U.S. troops had been attacked for 25 hours straight. But, they had not been defeated. The British gave up. They stopped their attack and withdrew from the battle at 7:30 a.m.

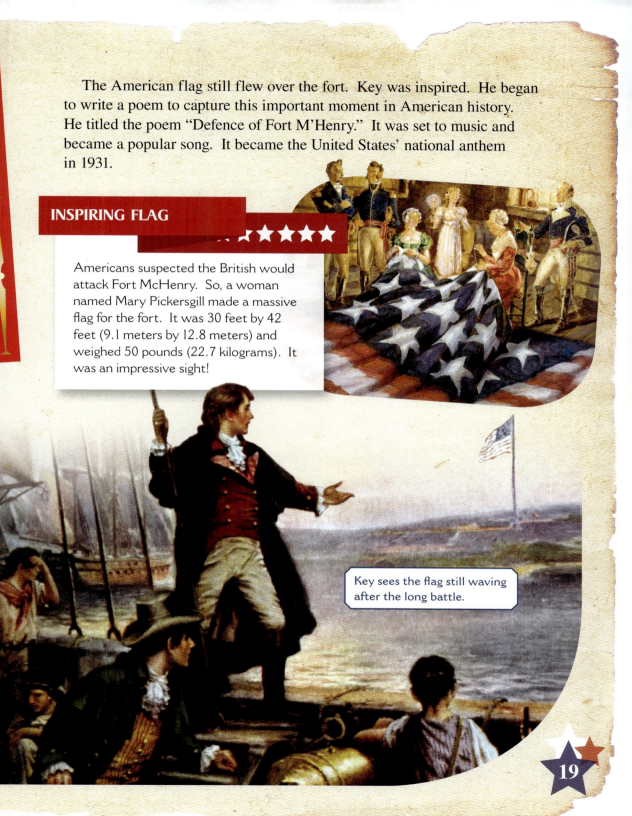

The American flag still flew over the fort. Key was inspired. He began to write a poem to capture this important moment in American history. He titled the poem "Defence of Fort M'Henry." It was set to music and became a popular song. It became the United States' national anthem in 1931.

INSPIRING FLAG

Americans suspected the British would attack Fort McHenry. So, a woman named Mary Pickersgill made a massive flag for the fort. It was 30 feet by 42 feet (9.1 meters by 12.8 meters) and weighed 50 pounds (22.7 kilograms). It was an impressive sight!

Key sees the flag still waving after the long battle.

Ending the War

Peace talks took place in Ghent, Belgium. They ended in December 1814, when the United States and Great Britain signed a **treaty** on Christmas Eve. It was called the Treaty of Peace and Amity between His Britannic Majesty and the United States of America. It is also known as the Treaty of Ghent.

The peace treaty focused on ending the war. It ordered a return to life the way it was before the war began. It said that territories, places, and possessions won during the war had to be returned.

the Treaty of Ghent

UNFAIR AGREEMENT ★★★★★

After the war, American Indians lost much of their land. The Treaty of Ghent ordered that tribal land be returned. But, there were no maps that showed the boundaries for this land, and the British and the Americans weren't interested in figuring it out.

The treaty did not solve all of the problems that caused the war in the first place. It did not order Great Britain to stop impressing sailors, for example. Sailors could still be taken from U.S. ships and forced to serve in the Royal Navy. The treaty also did not declare a winner or loser. The war ended in a **stalemate**.

Still, the United States won an important victory when the treaty was signed. The British finally accepted the United States as an independent country.

Leaders from the United States and Great Britain sign the Treaty of Ghent.

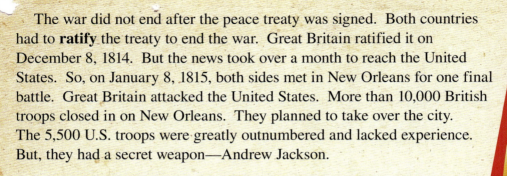

The war did not end after the peace treaty was signed. Both countries had to **ratify** the treaty to end the war. Great Britain ratified it on December 8, 1814. But the news took over a month to reach the United States. So, on January 8, 1815, both sides met in New Orleans for one final battle. Great Britain attacked the United States. More than 10,000 British troops closed in on New Orleans. They planned to take over the city. The 5,500 U.S. troops were greatly outnumbered and lacked experience. But, they had a secret weapon—Andrew Jackson.

Jackson was a **strategic** planner. His army lacked experience in battle. It was mostly made up of volunteers, free black men, and even a few pirates. And, they were outnumbered two to one. But Jackson helped his troops protect and defend themselves. They built a long barrier made of dirt and fought from behind it. When British troops approached, U.S. forces fired rifles and cannons. They killed or wounded about 2,600 British troops. With fewer than 100 lives lost, the United States won the battle.

Congress ratified the Treaty of Ghent on February 16, 1815. President Madison declared the war finally over.

GENERAL JACKSON

Major General Andrew Jackson led the army in the Battle of New Orleans. After the battle, he gained the respect of many Americans. In 1828, he ran for president and won. He served two terms as president.

Andrew Jackson and his troops win the final battle of the War of 1812.

After the War

Americans were in a **patriotic** mood after the War of 1812. The country was more independent than ever. The economy thrived. Because trade with Great Britain had been banned during the war, Americans began making goods themselves. As a result, factories grew.

The country itself grew, too. Great Britain was no longer involved with Eastern tribes. The British did not need them to help fight. The United States moved forward with earlier plans. It expanded into tribal lands. Sadly, this meant that many tribes had to give up their land and move west.

The war had an effect on other countries, too. Canada was more patriotic after the war. Settlers in Canada had fought to defend their home. They felt a new connection to the country. Canada later won its independence from British rule in 1867.

Great Britain moved on after the war. The British defeated Napoleon in the Battle of Waterloo. It was a great victory for them. It overshadowed earlier losses on U.S. soil.

Americans celebrate after Jackson's Victory in New Orleans.

24

Battle of Waterloo

Paying Tribute

In "The Star-Spangled Banner," Francis Scott Key calls the United States, "The land of the free and the home of the brave." He describes a flag that flies over a battle. It is a proud symbol of the nation. It stands for American values.

The War of 1812 began when Americans felt their values were threatened. They wanted their freedom. They wanted to prove their independence. Americans were not under British rule anymore. They were willing to fight for their beliefs.

The United States fought battles that seemed doomed for failure. It suffered crushing defeats. But, it had victories, too. Many gave their lives in these battles that helped shape the future of the country.

The United States was not declared the winner when the War of 1812 ended. But, it won what really mattered to Americans. The nation won proof of its freedom. "The Star-Spangled Banner" pays tribute to that victory.

Battle of New Orleans

the original flag that flew over Fort McHenry during the War of 1812

ORIGINS OF UNCLE SAM

★★★★★

During the War of 1812, a military supplier named Samuel Wilson sent food in barrels to soldiers. The barrels were marked "U.S." for "United States." People said the letters stood for "Uncle Sam." Over time, Uncle Sam became a symbol of the U.S. government.

Write It!

A flag inspired the writing of the American national anthem. The flag served as a symbol of freedom, hope, and victory.

Any object can have symbolic meaning. You may own some objects with symbolic meanings. You might have a ticket from a special event or a medal that you earned. Or, maybe you kept a special toy for years because it was your favorite. These items can symbolize the feelings you had during different times in your life.

Choose a keepsake that you saved for symbolic reasons. Write the memories and feelings it symbolizes. Then, use your notes to write a poem about the item.

Glossary

acquisition—the act of gaining something

allies—people who join together for a common cause or goal

anthem—a song of loyalty or praise

casualties—people who are hurt or killed during an accident or war

citizens—people who live in a country and have rights of that country

civilians—people who are not part of the military

court-martialed—sent to a military court trial

deserted—left a group without intending to return

detained—kept someone in one place

dictator—a person who rules a country with total authority and often in a cruel way

economy—the system of buying and selling goods and services

embargo—a government order that limits trade

expulsion—the act of forcing someone to leave

impressment—to seize and put someone into public service

invade—to forcefully enter a place in order to seize and conquer it

neutral—the act of not favoring or siding with someone during times of war

patriotic—to demonstrate love and loyalty to a country

ratify—make official by signing or voting

stalemate—a situation in which neither side can win

strategic—relating to a careful plan of action to achieve a goal

treaty—a formal agreement made between two or more countries or groups

Index

Your Turn!

An Inspiring Poem

This is the original draft of the poem Key wrote during the War of 1812. He titled it, "Defence of Fort M'Henry," though we now know it as, "The Star-Spangled Banner." The United States' national anthem is just one verse of Key's original poem. Research the rest of the poem and read the words carefully. Then, rewrite Key's poem in your own words, while keeping the original meaning.